A HEAD STA
Study Tips for the Student of

WESTERN CIVILIZATION:
A BRIEF HISTORY

VOLUME I: To 1715

Jackson J. Spielvogel
The Pennsylvania State University

Prepared by
James T. Baker
Western Kentucky University

West/Wadsworth
I⊤P® An International Thomson Publishing Company

Belmont, CA • Albany, NY • Boston • Cincinnati • Johannesburg • London • Madrid • Melbourne
Mexico City • New York • Pacific Grove, CA • Scottsdale, AZ • Singapore • Tokyo • Toronto

Cover Image: *A thirteenth-century miniature depicting the siege and capture of Constantinople by the fourth crusade in 1204*, by permission of Bibliotheque Nationale, Paris.

Printed in Canada.
  3 4 5 6 7 8 9 10

For more information, contact Wadsworth Publishing Company, 10 Davis Drive, Belmont, CA 94002, or electronically at http://www.wadsworth.com.

International Thomson Publishing Europe
Berkshire House
168-173 High Holborn
London, WC1V 7AA, United Kingdom

Nelson ITP, Australia
102 Dodds Street
South Melbourne
Victoria 3205 Australia

Nelson Canada
1120 Birchmount Road
Scarborough, Ontario
Canada M1K 5G4

International Thomson Publishing Japan
Hirakawa-cho Kyowa Building, 3F
2-2-1 Hirakawa-cho
Chiyoda-ku
Tokyo 102, Japan

International Thomson Editores
Seneca, 53
Colonia Polanco
11560 México D.F. México

International Thomson Publishing Asia
60 Albert Street #15-01
Albert Complex
Singapore 189969

International Thomson Publishing Southern Africa
Building 18, Constantia Square
138 Sixteenth Road, P.O. Box 2459
Halfway House, 1685 South Africa

Senior Developmental Editor: Sharon Adams Poore
Editorial Assistant: Melissa Gleason
Ancillary Coordinator: Rita Jaramillo
Print Buyer: Judy Inouye

ISBN 0-534-56078-4

CONTENTS

PREFACE

This small booklet was designed to accompany your text *Western Civilization: A Brief History* by Jackson J. Spielvogel. I hope that it will give you a head start, a critical edge, toward success in your course. In it you will find four types of aids to help you master each chapter:

1.   A brief Outline to provide you with the broad scope of the chapter.
2.   Key Terms to identify—the most important persons, places, events, ideas, and works of art, literature, and music of each period.
3.   Questions for Critical Thought—questions that ask you to interpret and relate factual materials: important in preparing for essay examinations.
4.   Questions on the Primary Source Documents—questions that ask you to apply the information provided in the boxes of each chapter to the age from which they come.

As you begin this course, you might keep in mind a few simple hints gathered from teachers and former students in this course on how to study:

1.   Read before attending each class the text material that will be covered. Your instructor will provide you with a syllabus making clear what pages you should read.
2.   Study for relatively short periods (30-45 minutes) several times a week rather than waiting for long free periods. Read your text slowly and carefully, making yourself notes in the margins, and do not skip around from place to place.
3.   Once a week rewrite the notes you have taken in class. Notes can grow "cold" if left as they were taken for too long a time; and only "warm notes," ones that make sense, can help you on examinations.
4.   First master the big picture in each section, using the Outlines provided in this booklet; and then master the smaller details, using the section with Key Terms.
5.   Ask yourself questions about the material, using both the Questions for Critical Thought and the Questions on the Documents.

Teachers and former students have also offered a few tips on how to perform well in class:

1.   Be on time. Not only does this make the right impression on your instructor, but it prevents you from missing vital information about future classes, assignments, and examinations which are often given at the beginning of classes.

2. Sit near the front. Studies have shown that those students who make the effort to sit close to the instructor hear better, see better, and remain more alert than those who sit further back.

3. Do not sit with close friends. Many people feel that friends provide support, both emotional and educational, but friends can also distract you. If you sit with friends, be sure they understand that they must not take your mind off the central purpose for being there: to see, hear, and learn the material.

4. Be rested when you come to class, stay alert, and take good notes. What happens in class is at least half of the course; and you should get as much from class lectures as possible. Do not feel that you have to take down the instructor's words verbatim. So long as you get the basic meaning, you will be in good shape.

5. Should you have any kind of learning disability, talk with your instructor at the beginning of the course. Most instructors are willing to provide whatever additional help you may need; and you should not wait or hesitate to take advantage of this help.

The scores you make on tests will likely be the largest factor in determining the grade you make in this course; and so it is important that you do well on examinations. Here too are a few hints:

1. Study regularly between examinations, not just the night before each one. If you have prepared all along the way, you need not "pull an all-nighter" in order to be ready. In fact, the all-nighter can do more harm than good. Being rested is vital to good performance on tests.

2. As soon as you are given your test, look it over quickly, get an idea of its scope, and judge how much time you will need to complete each part.

3. You will often be asked to identify persons, places, and events. Determine quickly how much time you have to identify each item, then give the basic facts about it but also its significance to the period you are studying. This added interpretive statement will demonstrate your superiority to the person with only superficial knowledge of the material.

4. If your test asks you to match items, whether persons, concepts, or definitions, complete the ones you know before returning to any you may not be sure you know. Matching the ones you know will give you confidence, and by the process of elimination you may identify some you did not at first see.

5. The same is true if you have to use a list of terms to fill in blanks. First use the ones you know, and you may then see better how to use those that remain.

You will probably be asked on your examinations to write essays. Essays not only test your knowledge of the facts but your ability to interpret and apply them. The exercises called Questions for Critical Thought and Questions on the Documents should be of help to you in preparing for essay questions. In addition let me offer you several suggestions on how to write essays that will both teach you and help you make high marks:

1. Read the entire question, and be sure that you understand exactly what is being asked and that you consider all parts of it. Address yourself only to the question that is asked, but address yourself to every section of it.

2. Make an outline before you begin to write the essay. Jot down in as few words as possible the major points you want to make, the most important persons, places, and ideas you want to include. Then glance back at your outline as you write so that you will not stay too long on one point or omit another.

3. Try to make one major point in your essay, with all of the others subordinate to it. This is your thesis. State it at the beginning, refer back to it at various appropriate times, and restate it briefly at the end. This will keep you focused on a unifying theme.

4. Write for an imaginary reader (who will be your teacher or an assistant, but you may not know exactly who it will be) who is intelligent but does not necessarily know the information you are relating. This way you will not fail to provide all information necessary to explain yourself, but you will also not insult your reader.

5. Be careful to spell correctly and to use good grammar. A history course is not an English course, and graders may or may not "count off" for poor spelling and grammar; but all graders are impressed either positively or negatively by the quality of your mechanics. While you may not see a specific comment about such matters on your essay, you may be sure that they have affected your final grade.

6. Think of an essay in a positive light. It should and can be an exercise in which the facts you have learned take focus and shape and make more sense than ever before. If done correctly, an essay can be the truest learning experience you can have and the most certain measure of your achievement.

I hope that this booklet adds to your enjoyment of the study of *Western Civilization*, increases your understanding of the ages you study, and helps you achieve high marks. I want to thank Elizabeth Jensen for her skill, accuracy, and speed in preparing it.

James T. Baker
Western Kentucky University

THE ANCIENT NEAR EAST: THE FIRST CIVILIZATIONS

Outline:

I. The First Humans
    A.   Hunter-Gatherers of the Old Stone Age
    B.   The Agricultural Revolution

II. The Emergence of Civilization
    A.   Urban Life
    B.   Religious Structures
    C.   Political and Military Structures
    D.   Socio-economic Structures
    E.   Writing
    F.   Artistic and Intellectual Activities
    G.   Material Objects

III. Civilization in Mesopotamia
    A.   City-States of Ancient Mesopotamia
    B.   Empires in Ancient Mesopotamia
    C.   The Code of Hammurabi
    D.   Mesopotamian Culture

IV. Egyptian Civilization
    A.   The Nile
    B.   Natural Barriers
    C.   The Old and Middle Kingdoms
    D.   Social and Economic Structures
    E.   Egyptian Culture
    F.   Chaos and a New Order
    G.   Daily Life in Ancient Egypt

Key Terms:

1.	Mesopotamia	MESS-OH-POE-*TAME*-EE-YA
2.	Hammurabi	HAM-YOUR-*OB*-EE
3.	Ziggurat	*ZIG*-UR-RAT
4.	Amon-Re	UH-MON-*RAY*
5.	Hieroglyphics	HIRE-UH-*GLIF*-IKS
6.	Aton	UH-*TAHN*

Questions for Critical Thought:

1.   What are the main characteristics of a civilization? What are its alternatives? Why do people or humans prefer civilization to its alternatives?

2.   Describe the economic and social structures of Mesopotamian civilization. How did geography help mold them? What legacies did they leave the world?

3.   Describe the Code of Hammurabi. What problems did it address, and what penalties did it impose on those who caused problems? In what ways would a modern person find it just and/ or unjust?

4.   In what ways was Egyptian religion molded by the geography of the land? Why did one form of religion find favor among the royal family, while quite another was popular with the masses?

5.   Describe daily life in Egypt: working, living in a family, worship. In what ways would you want and not want to live in that culture?

Questions on the Documents:

1.   What do the twelve laws from the Code of Hammurabi tell us about the nature and concerns of this king and his people? Why is this code said to based on the principle of "an eye for an eye?"

2.   Compare the flood story of Gilgamesh to the more familiar Biblical account. How does the Biblical account follow and how does it deviate from the older story?

3.   Use the "Hymn to the Nile" to show the importance of that river to Egypt. To what degree do the Egyptians consider it divine? Speculate on how the "Hymn to Pharaoh" might have been performed. Where, by whom, and in what dramatic form would it have been sung and acted?

4.   Describe the characteristics Egyptian officials were expected to exhibit. What sort of young man would have taken this kind of fatherly advice?

2 THE ANCIENT NEAR EAST: EMPIRES AND PEOPLES

Outline:

I.   On the Fringes of Civilization
    A.   Megaliths
    B.   Impact of Indo-Europeans: The Hittites

II.   The Hebrews: "The Children of Israel"
    A.   Moses, Solomon, and the Two Kingdoms
    B.   Spiritual Israel

III. The Phoenicians
    A.   Explorers to the West
    B.   Inventors of the Alphabet

IV.   The Assyrian Empire
    A.   Ashurbanipal
    B.   Military Superiority
    C.   Society and Culture

V.   The Persian Empire
    A.   Babylon and Nebuchadnezzar
    B.   Cyrus the Great
    C.   Darius
    D.   Governing the Empire
    E.   Persian Religion: Zoroaster

Key Terms:

1.	Exodus	*EKS*-OH-DUSS
2.	Covenant	*CUV*-AH-NUNT
3.	Yahweh	*YAW*-WAY
4.	Prophecy	*PRAH*-FA-CEE
5.	Ashurbanipal	ASH-UR-*BAN*-EE-PALL
6.	Satrapies	*SA*-TRA-PEAS
7.	Zoroaster	ZOH-ROH-*ASS*-TUR
8.	Ahuramazda	UH-HOOR-AH-*MAZZ*-DAH

Questions for Critical Thought:

1. In what ways was the Hebrew faith unique, and what characteristics did it share with neighboring religions?

2. Describe the political, military, and social organization of the Assyrian Empire. What influences did it have on subsequent middle eastern empires?

3. In what ways does the Persian emperor Cyrus deserve to be called by historians "the Great"?

4. Describe Zoroaster's religion. How did it change over time and spread from Persia to other nations? Do any of its principles survive in modern religions?

Questions on the Documents:

1. Describe the covenant Moses declared between Yahweh and Israel. What were the long-term implications for each side?

2. What did the Hebrew prophets say would happen if God's chosen people did not fulfill their obligations under the covenant? In what sense, then, were the Hebrews "chosen"?

3.   Describe the various Assyrian battle techniques. To what extent do you feel the official claims are exaggerated? What would be the purpose of such exaggeration?

4.   Pretend you are a modern reporter who has been permitted to return through time to cover a Persian king's banquet. Describe to your twentieth-century readers what you see.

THE CIVILIZATION OF THE GREEKS

Outline:

I.   Early Greece (Before 1100 B.C.)
    A.   Mountains and Sea
    B.   Crete and the Minoan Civilization
    C.   The Mycenaean Greeks

II.   The Greeks in a Dark Age (1100-750 B.C.)
    A.   The Dorians
    B.   Homer's Stories of Glory: *Iliad* and *Odyssey*

III.   The World of the Greek City-States (750-500 B.C.)
    A.   The Polis
    B.   Colonization and the Rise of Tyrants
    C.   The Example of Sparta
    D.   The Example of Athens

IV.   Classical Greece (500-338 B.C.)
    A.   The Persian Challenge
    B.   The Athenian Empire
    C.   The Peloponnesian War (431-404 B.C.)
    E.   The Culture of Classical Greece

Key Terms:

1.   Mycenae   MY-*SEE*-NEE

2.   Polis   *POH*-LISS

3.	Thermopylae	THUR-*MOP*-OH-LEE
4.	Thucydides	THOO-*SID*-UH-DEES
5.	Aeschylus	*ESS*-KU-LUS
6.	Socrates	*SOCK*-RAH-TEEZ
7.	Aristotle	*AIR*-ISS-TOT-UL
8.	Delphic Oracle	*DEL*-FIK *ORE*-UH-KUL

Questions for Critical Thought:

1. Discuss the importance of the writer Homer for the intellectual development of the Greeks. What was his description of the ideal Greek warrior?

2. Compare and contrast the development and characteristics of the two greatest Greek city-states, Athens and Sparta. Show how each became what it was and what each contributed to Greek culture.

3. Compare the origins, development, and characteristics of Greek tragedy and comedy.

4. Discuss the contributions of Plato and Aristotle to the development of Greek philosophy.

5. Outline the contributions of Herodotus and Thucydides in the development of the science of history.

Questions on the Documents:

1. What are the characteristics of the ideal Greek male as exemplified by Hector in the *Iliad*?

2. Show how being masters of a slave people who outnumbered them affected the development of the Spartans and their institutions, as illustrated by the Lycurgan Reforms.

3. In his funeral oration, Pericles clearly articulated the virtues of democracy. What are they? Are they relevant today?

4.   Discuss the way the Greek comedian Aristophanes used sex both as a comedic device and as a way of making a social statement.

5.   Using Xenophon as your guide and example, compare and contrast the role of women in Greek society to that in our own.

4 THE HELLENISTIC WORLD

Outline:

I.   The Rise of Macedonia and the Conquests of Alexander
       A.   Philip II and the Greeks
       B.   Alexander the Great
       C.   Alexander's Legacy: the Hellenistic World

II.   The World of the Hellenistic Kingdoms
       A.   The Antigonids of Macedonia
       B.   The Seleucids of Syria
       C.   The Ptolemids of Egypt
       D.   Hellenistic Cities
       E.   Economic and Social Trends

III.   Culture in the Hellenistic World
       A.   The Library of Alexandria
       B.   Hellenistic Literature
       C.   A Golden Age of Science and Medicine
       D.   Philosophy: New Schools of Thought

IV.   Religion in the Hellenistic World
       A.   Olympian Decline
       B.   Eastern Cults
       C.   Mystery Cults and Personal Salvation
       D.   The Jews

Key Terms:

1.	Demosthenes	DEE-*MOS*-THEN-EEZ
2.	Theocritus	THEE-*AH*-KRIT-US
3.	Menander	MEE-*NAN*-DER
4.	Polybius	POH-*LIB*-EE-US
5.	Euclid	*YOU*-KLID
6.	Archimedes	ARK-UH-*MEE*-DEEZ
7.	Epicurus	EP-EE-*CURE*-US
8.	Zeno	*ZEE*-NOH

Questions for Critical Thought:

1. What did Alexander's conquest do to the civilized world? How was this done?

2. List the characteristics of the typical Hellenistic city, and show how it transmitted Greek culture to the people around it.

3. It has been said that the Hellenistic age was a time of unusual scientific achievement. Explain how and why this is true.

4. Describe Hellenistic religion. What does it tell you about Hellenistic society, its concerns, its dreams?

Questions on the Documents:

1. Summarize briefly the two versions of why Alexander burned the Persian royal buildings. Using Arrian and Diodorus as starting points, try to reconstruct what really happened.

2. What do the two letters tell us about the status of Hellenistic women? To what extent can we say that this was a time of confusion in roles?

3.   Although little is known about the life of Hellenistic poet Theocritus, what can you tell of his interest and values from his *Seventh Idyll*?

4.   Recount as many principles of Stoicism as you can find in Cleanthes' *Hymn to Zeus*. To what class in society do you feel these ideals would most appeal? Why?

THE ROMAN REPUBLIC

Outline:

I.   The Emergence of Rome
    A.   Geography of the Italian Peninsula
    B.   The Greeks and Etruscans
    C.   Early Rome

II. The Roman Republic
    A.   Politics and Society in Rome—to 264 B.C.
    B.   The Roman Conquest of Italy

III. The Roman Conquest of the Mediterranean (264-133 B.C.)
    A.   Struggles with Carthage—the Punic Wars
    B.   The Eastern Mediterranean
    C.   The Nature of Roman Imperialism

IV. Society and Culture in the Roman Republic
    A.   Roman Religion
    B.   Slavery
    C.   The Family
    D.   Law
    E.   Literature and Art

V.   Decline and Fall of the Republic (133-31 B.C.)
    A.   Social, Economic, and Political Problems
    B.   The Reforms of Tiberius and Gaius Gracchus
    C.   Marius and Sulla
    D.   Collapse of the Republic

Key Terms:

1.	*Paterfamilias*	PAH-TER-FAM-*EE*-LEE-US
2.	Hannibal	*HAN*-UH-BUL
3.	Cato	*KAY*-TOH
4.	Livy	*LIVE*-EE
5.	Marius	*MAR*-EE-OOS
6.	Sulla	*SUL*-LAH
7.	Caesar	*SEE*-ZAR
8.	Cleopatra	KLEE-OH-*PAT*-RAH

Questions for Critical Thought:

1. How did the Etruscans and Greeks influence the early development of Rome's culture and politics? What was Etruscan and Greek about the Roman Republic?

2. Discuss the causes and results of the Punic Wars between Rome and Carthage. How did they help bring about the Roman Empire?

3. Describe the Roman family. Show how it proved an aid to Roman stability and conquest.

4. Show how the Romans tried to prop up their republic and how these efforts only hastened the coming of the empire.

Questions on the Documents:

1. Using Livy's account of Cincinnatus, describe the Roman ideal of the patriotic citizen-leader. How did such ideals contribute to Rome's successes?

2. Describe the Roman destruction of Carthage, and show what moral lessons some Romans drew from it.

3.   If we suppose Cato the Elder spoke for traditional Roman males, what do you see as their attitude toward women? Did this attitude make Rome stronger or weaker than it would have been with different attitudes?

4.   Describe the assassination of Julius Caesar, and point out the facts presented by Plutarch which a playwright 1000 years later might use for dramatic effect.

6 THE ROMAN EMPIRE

Outline:

I. The Age of Augustus (31 B.C.-14 A.D.)
- A. The New Order
- B. The Army of Augustus
- C. Augustan Society

II. The Early Empire
- A. Julio-Claudian (14-69) and Flavian (69-96) Emperors
- B. The Five "Good Emperors" (96-180)
- C. The Empire at its Height
- D. Prosperity
- E. Culture and Society

III. Religion in the Roman World
- A. The Religious World of the Empire
- B. The Jews
- C. The Rise of Christianity

IV. The Decline and Fall of Rome
- A. Military Monarchy
- B. Invasions and Civil Wars
- C. Diocletian and Constantine
- D. Growth of Christianity
- E. The Fall of the Western Roman Empire

Key Terms:

1. Augustus   AW-*GUST*-US

2.	Nero	*NEE*-ROH
3.	Hadrian	*HAY*-DREE-UHN
4.	Seneca	*SIN*-IK-KAH
5.	Tacitus	*TASS*-UH-TUSS
6.	Mithras	MYTH-*RUSS*
7.	Diocletian	DIO-OH-*KLEE*-SHUN
8.	Visigoths	*VIZ*-UH-GOTHS

Questions for Critical Thought:

1. Discuss the way Augustus Caesar ruled his new empire, particularly how he organized his government and used his army. To what extent did his policies assure the empire's long-term survival?

2. What were the major interests and concerns of the writers of Rome's Golden and Silver Ages? What forms did their responses to these interests and concerns take?

3. What did the "five good emperors" contribute to the development of the Roman Empire? Why were their policies not effectively continued after them?

4. Discuss the significance of St. Paul for the development of the Christian faith. Why is he called the "second founder" of Christianity?

5. Why did Rome fall? Are there "lessons" in this story for modern societies and governments?

Questions on the Documents:

1. Show how the famous inscription *Res Gestae* is both history and propaganda.

2. Discuss the probable appearance and personality of a Roman who often attended the banquets of the upper classes.

3. Describe Ovid's theories of love and why the moralistic Augustus found them offensive.

4.   Tell what it was like to go to a Roman bath, and show why these places were so popular. Why would you or would you not be a participant?

5.   Pretend you have just read the Sermon on the Mount by the obscure Jewish teacher, Jesus of Nazareth, for the first time. What would be your estimate of the man who spoke these words?

THE PASSING OF THE ROMAN WORLD AND THE EMERGENCE OF MEDIEVAL CIVILIZATION

Outline:

I.   The Transformation of the Roman World: The Role of the Germanic Peoples
    A.   Ostrogoths in Italy: Theodoric
    B.   Visigoths in Spain
    C.   The Frankish Kingdom
    D.   Anglo-Saxon England
    E.   Germanic Society
    F.   The Frankish Family and Marriage

II.   The Role and Development of the Christian Church
    A.   Church Organization and Early Religious Disputes
    B.   The Power of the Pope
    C.   Monks and their Mission
    D.   Christianity and Intellectual Life

III.   The Byzantine Empire
    A.   The Reign of Justinian (527-565)
    B.   From Eastern Roman to Byzantine Empire

IV.   The Rise of Islam
    A.   Arabia Before Muhammad
    B.   Muhammad
    C.   The Expansion of Islam

Key Terms:

1.   Theodoric   THEE-ODD-*OR*-IK

2.   *Wergeld*   *WUR*-GELD

3.   Benedict   *BEN*-EE-DIKT

4.   Augustine   AW-*GUSS*-TIN

5.   Justinian   JUSS-*TINN*-EE-UN

6.   Vulgate   *VUL*-GIT

7.   Hagia Sophia   *HAG*-EE-AH   SOH-*FEE*-AH

8.   Allah   *AH*-LUH

Questions for Critical Thought:

1.   Discuss the monastic movement that swept the church in the first few centuries after Christ. What did its life offer young people in a world that seemed to be falling apart?

2.   Outline the part played by monks in the conversion of Europe to Christianity. Give examples using the more prominent ones, and show what they accomplished.

3.   How did the Eastern empire (Byzantium) differ from the tribal societies that replaced the Western empire at the other end of the Mediterranean? Was East or West truer to the Roman model?

4.   Describe the religion and culture of Islam. Discuss its origins, its conquest of a large part of the civilized world, and its immediate and permanent impact on civilization.

Questions on the Documents:

1.   Describe the Germanic "ordeal" and speculate on the logic of it. What kind of society would choose it as a way to achieve justice? Is it part of our modern legal system in modified form?

2.   If the spiritual biographies of early Christian monks were meant to inspire model behavior in the average Christian, what personal characteristics would the life of St. Anthony have taught readers to imitate?

3.   After reading Cummean, what conclusions can you draw about early Irish Christianity's philosophy of human sexuality? Was it healthy? Explain.

4.   To what extent was Islam, in its early days, a radical and militant faith? Why and how did Muhammad establish Allah as the moral authority for his teachings?

CHAPTER

8 EUROPEAN CIVILIZATION IN THE EARLY MIDDLE AGES, 750-1000

Outline:

I. The World of the Carolingians
   A. The Role of Pepin
   B. Charlemagne and the Carolingian Empire (768-814)
   C. The Carolingian Intellectual Renewal
   D. Life in the Carolingian World

II. The Disintegration of the Carolingian Empire
   A. Division of the Empire
   B. Invasions of the Ninth and Tenth Centuries

III. The Emerging World of Feudalism
   A. The Feudal System: Lords and Vassals
   B. The Manorial System

IV. The Zenith of Byzantine Civilization
   A. The Reign of Michael III (842-867) and the Photian Schism
   B. The Macedonian Rulers

V. The Slavic Peoples of Central and Eastern Europe
   A. Conversion to Christianity
   B. Divisions Within the Language Group
   C. The Rus of Kiev and Vladimir

VI. The World of Islam
   A. The Abbasid Dynasty
   B. Islamic Civilization

Key Terms:

1. Pepin   *PEP*-INN

2. *Missi Dominici*   *MISS*-EE DOME-IN-*EE*-SEE

3. Einhard   *INE*-HART

4. Vassalage   *VASS*-UL-AGE

5. Fief   *FEEF*

6. Subinfeudation   SUB-IN-FYOOD-*A*-CHUN

7. Vladimir   *VLAHD*-U-MEER

8. Avicenna   AV-UH-*SEE*-NAH

Questions for Critical Thought:

1. What was the significance for subsequent Western European civilization of Charlemagne's interest in education and classical learning?

2. What surprised you about the diet and hygiene of the various classes in the Carolingian era? What did not surprise you?

3. Discuss the system known as feudalism. Show how it responded to and attempted to solve the social problems of its day. In what ways did it succeed and in what ways did it fail?

4. Discuss the relationship of the Slavic peoples of Eastern Europe to the Germanic peoples of Western Europe in their formative days. How do those relationships continue today, and what are the consequences?

Questions on the Documents:

1. Show how Einhard portrayed Charlemagne as the ideal leader. To what extent does his portrayal seem exaggerated?

2.   Describe the way a young man called to serve an early medieval king was supposed to conduct himself. Why at this time might a mother be the one to teach her son these lessons?

3.   Recount the visit of Liudprand of Cremona to the Byzantine court of Constantine VII. Explain why future historians, reading such accounts, would give the adjective "Byzantine" its modern connotation.

4.   Summarize Ibn Fadlan's impressions of the Rus he met. What did he find offensive, and what do such things tell us about the Muslim society from which he came?

THE RECOVERY AND GROWTH OF EUROPEAN SOCIETY IN THE HIGH MIDDLE AGES

Outline:

I. People and Land in the High Middle Ages
   A. A Dramatic Increase in Population and a Decline in Slavery
   B. The New Agriculture
   C. Daily Life of the Peasantry

II. The Recovery and Reform of the Catholic Church
   A. The Problem of Decline
   B. The Cluniac Reform Movement
   C. Reform of the Papacy
   D. Gregory VII and the Investiture Controversy

III. Christianity and Medieval Civilization
   A. Growth of the Papal Monarchy
   B. New Religious Orders and Spiritual Ideals
   C. Popular Religion
   D. Voices of Protest and Intolerance

Key Terms:

1. Cluny   *KLOO*-NEE

2. Investiture   IN-*VEST*-IT-TYUR

3. Cistercian   SIS-*TUR*-SHAN

4. Hildegard   *HILL*-DUH-GAHRD

5.	Dominic	*DAHM*-IN-IK
6.	Relic	*REL*-IK
7.	Albigensian	AL-BUH-*GEN*-SEE-YAN
8.	Ghetto	*GET*-TOH

Questions for Critical Thought:

1.   Recount the story of the Investiture Controversy. What caused it, and what were its short and long term results?

2.   What role did women play in the religious life of the Middle Ages? What conclusions can you draw from this role about the age in which these women lived?

3.   Show how the reign of Innocent III illustrates religious power politics. What kind of churchman succeeded in his day?

4.   What was the "Holy Office"? Why was it established, and what did it accomplish? Can you name any similar institutions in the twentieth century?

Questions on the Documents:

1.   What does the story of Abbot Suger and his timbers tell you about the treatment of forests and other natural resources, both by warriors and clergymen, during the Middle Ages?

2.   Describe the tone of Pope Gregory's account of his confrontation with Henry IV. In what sense was this pope truly a prince among princes? How did his power differ from that of other rulers?

3.   Recount one of the miracles attributed to Saint Bernard. Other than demonstrating his saintliness, what is the story's theme?

4.   What seems to have been the typical Christian opinion of Jews in the Middle Ages? How did such opinions form? What were the results?

A NEW WORLD OF CITIES AND KINGDOMS

Outline:

I. The New World of Trade and Cities
  A. The Revival of Trade
  B. The Growth of Cities
  C. Life in the Medieval City
  D. Industry in Medieval Cities

II. The Aristocracy of the High Middle Ages
  A. Significance of Aristocracy
  B. Daily Life of the European Nobility

III. The Emergence and Growth of European Kingdoms (1000-1300)
  A. England: Normans and Plantagenets
  B. France and the Capetians
  C. Spain and Reconquest
  D. The Holy Roman Empire
  E. New Kingdoms in Eastern Europe
  D. The Development of Russia

Key Terms:

1. Burgher   *BURG*-UR

2. Chivalry   SHIV-*UL*-REE

3. Melee   *MAY*-LAY

4. Joust   *GOWST*

5.	*Magna Carta*	*MAG*-NUH *CART*-UH
6.	Parlement	PAR-LAY-*MOHN*
7.	Barbarossa	BAR-BAR-*OH*-SUH
8.	Genghis Khan	JEN-GIS-*KAHN*

Questions for Critical Thought:

1.   Describe the way a typical late medieval city was organized. Where did power lie, and who benefited from it?

2.   Discuss the effects of rapid population growth on late medieval economic and social development. What could have been done to modify the effects?

3.   Describe chivalry and the life of a young man being trained for military service to his lord. To what extent was it necessary for social stability, and to what extent was it all just fun and games?

4.   Compare the way various royal families consolidated their powers and show how each one created the later character of its nation.

Questions on the Documents:

1.   Compare and contrast medieval and modern pollution. How much more or less likely are we to solve our own problems of pollution than the King of England solved those of Boutham?

2.   What seems to have been the consensus among medieval men, as demonstrated by the two men you have read, about medieval women? What does this say about the men?

3.   Describe some of the rights King John of England granted his lords in *Magna Carta*. Show how these rights could later be expanded to help all Englishmen.

4.   What does the *Chronicle* of Helmhold tell us about German treatment of Slavs? How was the "ethnic cleansing" of that day accomplished?

CRUSADES AND CULTURE IN THE HIGH MIDDLE AGES

11

Outline:

I.   Background to the Crusades
    A.   The Islamic Empire
    B.   The Byzantine Empire

II.   The Crusades
    A.   Urban II at Clermont
    B.   Peter the Hermit and the "Peasant's Crusade"
    C.   The First Crusade
    D.   The Second Crusade: Bernard of Clairvaux
    E.   The Third Crusade: A "Crusade of Kings"
    F.   Crusades of the Thirteenth Century
    G.   Effects of the Crusades

III.   The Intellectual and Artistic World of the High Middle Ages
    A.   The Rise of Universities
    B.   The Renaissance of the Twelfth Century
    C.   Scholasticism
    D.   The Revival of Roman Law
    E.   Literature in the High Middle Ages
    F.   Romanesque Architecture
    G.   Gothic Cathedrals

Key Terms:

1.   Fatimids   *FAT*-UH-MIDZ

2.   Seljuk Turks   *SELL*-JUK   TERX

3.   Bernard of Clairvaux   *BURN*-URD OF KLAAR-*VOH*

4.	Paleologi	PALE-EE-*OL*-OH-GEE
5.	Aquinas	UK-*WINE*-US
6.	*Summa Theologica*	*SUUM*-AH TAY-OH-*LOGE*-I-KA
7.	Troubadour	*TROO*-BU-DOOR
8.	St. Denis	SAHN DEE-*NEE*

Questions for Critical Thought:

1.   What were the causes and results of the crusades? How did they change Europe?

2.   What were the concerns of theological philosophers in the Middle Ages? Name the major figures in this field and how they resolved the questions their concerns raised.

3.   Discuss the major interests of literature in the High Middle Ages. What forms and styles did writers use to express these interests?

4.   What does the Gothic cathedral tell us about late medieval values and science?

Questions on the Documents:

1.   What methods did Pope Urban II use to persuade churchmen to launch the First Crusade? Given his persuasive skills, what position would you give him in a modern corporation?

2.   Describe the conquest of Holy Jerusalem by the Christian crusaders. Under what system of ethics did they seem to be operating?

3.   Speculate on the conditions of life in a medieval university town that would lead to such riots as the one in Oxford. Which side was more at fault?

4.   What percentages of logic, authority, and contemporary prejudice make up Thomas Aquinas' conclusions about the formation of woman?

5.   Roland was a medieval hero and role model. From the famous song about his life, pick out the qualities medieval men obviously admired. How do they resemble and differ from qualities admired in men today?

CHAPTER

The Late Middle Ages: Crisis and Disintegration in the Fourteenth Century

12

Outline:

I.   A Time of Troubles: Black Death and Social Crisis
    A.   Famine and Population Decline
    B.   The Black Death
    C.   Economic Dislocation and Social Upheaval

II. War and Political Instability
    A.   The Hundred Years' War
    B.   Political Instability
    C.   England and France
    D.   The German Monarchy
    E.   The States of Italy

III. The Decline of the Church
    A.   Boniface VIII against Philip IV
    B.   The Avignon Papacy (1305-1378)
    C.   The Great Schism (1378-1415)
    D.   The Rise of Conciliarism

IV. Culture and Society in an Age of Diversity
    A.   Vernacular Literature
    B.   Art and the Black Death
    C.   Changes in Urban Life
    D.   Inventions of Note

Key Terms:

1.	Flagellant	*FLAGE*-ELL-ANT
2.	Pogrom	*POH*-GROM
3.	Ciompi	*CHOM*-PEE
4.	Agincourt	*AGE*-IN-CORE
5.	*Unam Sanctam*	*OON*-AHM *SANK*-TAHM
6.	Avignon	AH-VEEN-*YON*
7.	Conciliarism	KON-*SILL*-EE-ARE-ISIM
8.	Giotto	JAH-TOE

Questions for Critical Thought:

1. Why were there peasant revolts in the fourteenth century? What forms did they take in various countries? What did they achieve?

2. What caused the Church's Great Schism, and what effects did it have on late medieval religious life? How did the average Christian carry on his/her religious devotions during the period when the Church was in such a state of chaos?

3. Why did late medieval writers begin to use vernacular languages? What resulted from this decision?

4. How did the plague called the Black Death affect the late medieval medical profession?

Questions on the Documents:

1. Describe the effects of the Black Death on individuals and cities. Why was it often attributed to the wrath of God?

2. Explain how superstition, fear, prejudice, and greed combined to cause the attack upon European Jews in 1349.

3. Explain what would give a peasant girl like Joan of Arc the courage to follow the orders of her "voices" to death? What does this tell you about the medieval personality and its belief system?

4. Discuss the claims Pope Boniface VIII made for papal authority in *Unam Sanctam*. What does the fact that this declaration caused such violent reaction say about prior understandings of papal power?

5. In his *Comedy*, Dante used his ironic sense of humor to show how each sinner's punishment matched his sin. Use the case of Alessio Da Lucca to illustrate this point.

CHAPTER

13 RECOVERY AND REBIRTH: THE AGE OF THE RENAISSANCE

Outline:

I.   Meaning and Characteristics of the Italian Renaissance
   A.   An Urban Society
   B.   An Age of Recovery
   C.   A Rebirth of Classical Culture
   D.   Recovery of the Individual

II.   The Making of Renaissance Society
   A.   Economic Recovery
   B.   Social Changes

III.   The Italian States in the Renaissance
   A.   The Five Major States: Milan, Venice, Florence, the Papal States, and Naples
   B.   The Examples of Federigo da Montefeltro and Isabella d'Este
   C.   Machiavelli and the New Statecraft

IV.   The Intellectual Renaissance in Italy
   A.   Humanism
   B.   Humanism and Philosophy
   C.   Education
   D.   The Impact of Printing

V.   The Artistic Renaissance
   A.   The Early Renaissance
   B.   The High Renaissance
   C.   The Northern Artistic Renaissance

VI.   The European State in the Renaissance
    A.   The "New Monarchies"
    B.   Central Europe: The Holy Roman Empire
    C.   The Struggle for Strong Monarchy in Eastern Europe
    D.   The Ottoman Turks and the End of the Byzantine Empire

VII.   The Church in the Renaissance
    A.   The Problems of Heresy and Reform
    B.   The Renaissance Papacy

Key Terms:

1.   Castiglione   KAH-STEE-*LYOH*-NEE

2.   Isabella d'Este   EES-UH-*BELL*-UH   *DES*-TEE

3.   Machiavelli   MAK-EE-AH-*VELL*-EE

4.   Pico della Mirandola   *PEE*-KO   *DELL*-AH   MEER-*AND*-OH-LA

5.   Vittorino da Feltre   VEE-TOR-*EE*-NOH   DAH   *FELL*-TREE

6.   Masaccio   MU-*SAH*-CHEE-OH

7.   Leonardo da Vinci   LEE-UH-*NAR*-DOH   DAH   *VIN*-CHEE

8.   Michelangelo   MIKE-EL-*AN*-GU-LOW

Questions for Critical Thought:

1.   In what sense can it be said that Machiavelli created a new political science? Describe it. What message does it have for modern readers?

2.   Define Renaissance humanism. Name the leading humanists, and tell what they wanted to and actually did accomplish.

3.   How did humanism affect Renaissance theories and practices of education? Give examples. Are they still pertinent?

4.   Compare and contrast the Northern and Southern forms of Renaissance art. Which is now considered more universal in appeal? Why?

5.   What kind of pope did the Renaissance produce? How did these popes affect the Renaissance?

Questions on the Documents:

1.   What conclusions can be drawn about the wealthy Renaissance man's diet and probable health by perusing the menu from one of Pope Pius V's banquets? Do you consider it unseemly for a pope and his guests to enjoy such food? Why or why not?

2.   According to the letters of Alessandra Strozzi, what characteristics and advantages did a Renaissance family look for when searching out a wife for one of its sons? What kind of marriage would he likely have?

3.   What was Machiavelli's advice to a prince who wanted to hold power? Do you feel that he is serious or in any way being sarcastic?

4.   What was the Renaissance image of man? Use Pico della Mirandola's *Oration* to demonstrate what the humanists believed man's nature and potential to be.

CHAPTER

THE AGE OF REFORMATION

14

Outline:

I.   Prelude to Reformation
    A.   Christian (Northern Renaissance) Humanism
    B.   Erasmus and *The Praise of Folly*
    C.   Church and Religion on the Eve of the Reformation
    D.   Abuses of the Clergy
    E.   Popular Religion

II.   Martin Luther and the Reformation in Germany
    A.   The Early Luther
    B.   The Development of Lutheranism
    C.   Germany and the Reformation: Religion and Politics
        1.   Emperor Charles V's Attempt to Preserve Christian Unity
        2.   The Peace of Augsburg: The Success of Lutheranism

III. The Spread of the Protestant Reformation
    A.   Ulrich Zwingli in Switzerland
    B.   The Radical Reformation: The Anabaptists
    C.   The Reformation in England
    D.   Calvinism

IV.   The Social Impact of the Reformation
    A.   The Effect on Families
    B.   Religious Practices and Popular Culture

V.   The Catholic Reformation
    A.   Loyola and the Jesuits
    B.   A Revived Papacy
    C.   The Council of Trent

Key Terms:

1.	Thomas á Kempis	*TAHM*-US UH *KEMP*-US
2.	Indulgence	INN-*DULL*-GENZ
3.	Tetzel	*TET*-SELL
4.	Augsburg	*AHGS*-BURG
5.	Anabaptist	ANN-UH-*BAP*-TIST
6.	Predestination	PREE-DESS-TIN-*AY*-SHUN
7.	Jesuit	*JEZZ*-YOU-IT
8.	Matteo Ricci	MAH-*TAY*-OH *REECH*-EE

Questions for Critical Thought:

1.   Discuss the life and work of Desiderius Erasmus, showing his place in the Northern Renaissance and in preparing for the Reformation.

2.   Identify Martin Luther's part in the coming of the Protestant revolt. What personal qualities made Luther act as he did, and how did his actions affect the course of the Reformation?

3.   Discuss the Reformation in England. What caused it? How did it differ from the Reformation in other places? What were its results?

4.   Who was John Calvin, and what was Calvinism? Explain why and how he came to have such widespread influence in Protestantism?

5.   What shape did the Catholic Reformation take? How did the reformed Catholic Church differ from Protestantism? How well did its reforms prepare it for future ages?

Questions on the Documents:

1.   Show how and why Martin Luther's classroom exercise, The Ninety-Five Theses, caused such a sensation and had such an impact on his society and times.

2.   Using the Marburg Colloquy as your guide, draw as many conclusions as you can about Luther's personality, mind, and public manner.

3.   If Catherine Zell is typical of the Anabaptist faith, what new themes did this movement bring to Christianity? To what extent were these themes the natural consequences of Luther's doctrinal innovations?

4.   If one follows Loyola's formula for correct Christian thinking, what does the Christian believe? How does the Christian act? What does the Christian accomplish?

CHAPTER 15
DISCOVERY AND CRISIS IN THE SIXTEENTH AND SEVENTEENTH CENTURIES

Outline:

I. An Age of Discovery and Expansion
    A. The Motives Behind Them
    B. The Portuguese Maritime Empire
    C. Voyages to the New World
    D. The Spanish Empire
    E. Administration of the Empire
    F. The Impact of Expansion

II. Politics and Wars of Religion in the Sixteenth Century
    A. The French Wars of Religion (1562-1598)
    B. Philip II and Militant Catholicism
    C. Elizabeth's England

III. Economic and Social Crises
    A. Economic Declines
    B. The Witchcraft Craze

IV. Seventeenth-Century Crises: War and Rebellions
    A. The Thirty Years' War (1618-1648)
    B. Rebellions

V. Culture in a Turbulent World
    A. Art: Mannerism and Baroque
    C. A Golden Age of Literature

Key Terms:

1. Vasco da Gama   *VASS*-KOH DU *GAAM*-AH

2. *Encomienda*   INN-KOH-MEE-*INN*-DAH

3. Huguenot   *YOU*-GHEN-OH

4. Armada   ARE-*MAH*-DAH

5. Mannerism   *MAN*-UR-IZ-UM

6. Baroque   BAR-*OHK*

7. Bernini   *BURR*-NEE-NEE

8. Cervantes   SIR-*VAHN*-TEZ

Questions for Critical Thought:

1. Describe the empire which the Spanish established in the Americas: its government, its social and religious systems, its economy, its strengths and weaknesses.

2. In recounting the French religious wars, what peculiarly "French" characteristics do you find in them? What events in French history had helped create these characteristics?

3. Describe the Elizabethan religious settlement in England. Was the Church of England Protestant or Catholic? Why did it work so well?

4. Explain the witch hunt craze of the seventeenth century. What conditions fueled it, and why did it at long last end?

5. Compare the lives and achievements of Montaigne, Shakespeare, and Cervantes. What do these men's careers tell you about each one's country in the sixteenth and seventeenth centuries?

Questions on the Documents:

1.   What did Cortes think of the Aztec civilization he conquered? What does he indicate made him feel justified in destroying it? What does this say about his own Spanish civilization?

2.   From the witchcraft case you have read, what "rules" of law did the witch hunters of the seventeenth century follow? How would a modern defense attorney attack their case?

3.   Describe the treatment of peasants on the farm captured by foreign soldiers during the Thirty Years' War, as recounted in the novel *Simplicius Simplicissimus*. To what extent do you see exaggeration for effect, and to what extent does this account agree with what you have read of treatment of civilians in other wars?

4.   How much of Shakespeare's tribute to England in "Richard II" is patriotism, how much xenophobia, and how much the dramatist's wish to please his audience? Give examples of your opinion.

RESPONSE TO CRISIS: STATE BUILDING AND THE SEARCH FOR ORDER IN THE SEVENTEENTH CENTURY

Outline:

Key Terms:

1. Absolutism   AB-SOH-*LUTE*-IZ-IM

2. Richelieu   *RISH*-LOO

3. Fronde   *FROHND*

4. Colbert   KOLE-*BARE*

5.   Hohenzollerns   *HOE*-IN-ZOHL-URNS

6.   Habsburgs   *HABZ*-BERGZ

7.   *Leviathan*   LUH-*VYE*-UH-THUN

8.   Mercantilism   *MUR*-KAN-TEEL-IZ-UM

Questions for Critical Thought:

1.   List and explain the steps in Louis XIV's steady march toward absolute rule in France. What do you consider the most crucial steps for his eventual success?

2.   What factors transformed the rather unpromising German province of Brandenburg-Prussia into the core of what was to be a German nation? Explain each factor.

3.   Describe Peter Romanov's role in the emergence of modern Russia. Was he more or less important for Russia than Louis XIV was for France? Explain your answer.

4.   Describe the way a near-absolute monarchy became the world's first truly constitutional monarchy in Britain. What three persons do you feel contributed most to this change, and why?

5.   List and explain the new political theories that grew out of the Age of Absolutism. Show how each one was a product of its time.

Questions on the Documents:

1.   How do Louis XIV's *Memoirs* show that he had given some thought to the duties of a king? How well did his theory fit his actions?

2.   Explain how Peter Romanov's treatment of the rebellious Streltsy might demonstrate Machiavelli's notion that the effective ruler must act without consideration for the usual principles of morality.

3.   Explain how the 1688 British Bill of Rights paved the way for constitutional government. Show how this Bill influenced American colonists in the next century.

4.   How did Moliere satirize the world of scholarship? To what extent do you think his audience would have taken his joke seriously?

TOWARD A NEW HEAVEN AND A NEW EARTH: THE SCIENTIFIC REVOLUTION AND THE EMERGENCE OF MODERN SCIENCE

Outline:

V.   Toward a New Earth: Descartes, Rationalism, and a New View of Humankind
      A.   Descartes' *Discourse on Method*
      B.   The Implications of Cartesian Dualism

VI.   Science and Religion in the Seventeenth Century
      A.   The Example of Galileo
      B.   Blaise Pascal and His *Pensées*

VII. The Spread of Scientific Knowledge
      A.   Scientific Method: Bacon and Descartes
      B.   Scientific Societies
      C.   Science and Society

Key Terms:

1.   Hermetic   HUR-*MET*-IK

2.   Geocentric   GEE-OH-*SIN*-TRIK

3.   Heliocentric   HEEL-EE-OH-*SIN*-TRIK

4.   *Principia*   PRIN-*SIP*-EE-AH

5.   Vesalius   VUH-*SAIL*-EE-US

6.   Cartesian dualism   KAR-*TEEZ*-EE-UN *DEW*-AL-IZ-UM

7.   Spinoza   SPIN-*OH*-ZUH

8.   Pascal   PASS-*KAL*

Questions for Critical Thought:

1.   Discuss the causes of the Scientific Revolution of the seventeenth century. Of these causes, which seems the strangest to modern minds? Why?

2.   Discuss the men who added new knowledge to the field of medicine during the seventeenth century, and briefly describe each one's contribution to the field.

3.   Discuss the women who contributed to the Scientific Revolution, and briefly describe each one's contribution. Why did male scientists have such difficulties accepting them as equals?

4.   Describe the "scientific method," showing how you might use it to study a particular problem or question in a certain branch of science.

5.   How did the Scientific Revolution affect religious thought? How did religious thought affect the Revolution?

Questions on the Documents:

1.   Explain why Copernicus' heliocentric theory was at the same time so simple and so profound.

2.   What personality traits can you find in Galileo's account of his astronomical observations that would explain why he was a successful scientist?

3.   Speculate on why—amid the scientific progress of his century and despite evidence to the contrary—Spinoza was so unprepared to accept women as equals.

4.   What was at the root of Pascal's doubts about man's ability to find scientific certainty? What problems for future scientists did he accurately pose?